RENOIR

Renoir

BY BRUNO F. SCHNEIDER

CROWN PUBLISHERS INC. ▪ NEW YORK

Title Page: Self-Portrait with White Hat. 1910; 20″ × 16″
Durand-Ruel Collection, Paris - New York

Translated by:
DESMOND AND CAMILLE CLAYTON

PRINTED IN ITALY – INDUSTRIE GRAFICHE CATTANEO S.P.A., BERGAMO – © 1978 BY BONFINI PRESS S.A., NAEFELS, SWITZERLAND
ALL RIGHTS IN THE U.S.A. ARE RESERVED BY CROWN PUBLISHERS, INC., NEW YORK, N.Y.

REGATTA AT ARGENTEUIL. 1874; 12″ × 18″, Private Collection, Paris

« *Like a child, I paint before nature with an artless soul and the instincts of my fingertips* ».

PIERRE-AUGUSTE RENOIR

If such words were to be spoken in the middle of the 20th century they would sound, in relation to the the aims of our artists, objective or abstract, immodest, incredibly arrogant, for the words « an artless soul and the instincts of the fingertips » describe in simple terms the highest ideals of the painting of today, ideals, moreover, which are seldom attained. Renoir, however, did attain them. And yet these words were not the outcome of an artist's pride, but of a great and gentle modesty, a humbleness before the creation and its creatures, and before art. These words do not imply « I have achieved, » but « I was allowed to achieve ». Renoir was, after all, not an intellectual artist who strove to vitalize his work by means of reflected naivité, but a man who presented the world afresh, consonant with himself, his soul, and his ability. One hesitates to apply the word « genius » to him, because this word does not neces-

5

sarily imply the fecundity and simplicity which was Renoir's and which made his pictures resemble happy natural phenomena. There is no doubt, however, that he was a genius if one takes genius to comprise the powers of a pure and vital soul, and an inexhaustible creative urge.

Renoir said of himself once, half regretfully and half proudly: « I am like a small cork which has fallen into the water and is being carried away by the current. I surrender myself unconditionally to painting ». His genius consisted in the inexhaustibility of his visions which gently, but irresistibly, demanded expression. All the rest was craftsmanship: sterling craftsmanship and iron assiduity, for Renoir began as a craftsman, as a porcelain painter, and took the path of diligence to great art and fulfilment.

It is high time for the word colour to be mentioned, for to speak of Renoir is to speak of colour. It is true, of course, that all the Impressionists worshipped colour and light. In Renoir's pictures, however, they develop into ecstatic feasts, the light takes on material qualities, it foams and sparkles in his pictures, and sometimes illuminates the colours like precious stones. If one of his works were taken into a gallery of pictures by the official masters of the Ecole des Beaux-Arts of the 19th century, all the rest would dissolve into a dirty blackish brown, compared with Renoir's brilliant colours. Even the pictures by moderate revolutionaires, like those of Corot, with their silvery twilight, or of Daubigny, with their delicate, lustrous colours, fade into darkness before an early Renoir like *Lise* in the Folkwang Museum in Essen. And this despite the fact that in this picture he still has both feet planted firmly on the ground of tradition, and that colour was only to reach its full maturity in his later pictures, in which it seems to have become luminescent. There are no longer reflections of sunlight, which, in the early garden pictures, for example, were applied with thick strokes of the brush; now the paint has thinned, and the canvas appears to be transilluminated from behind. This paradise of colour, which surpasses all Impressionist theories, is Renoir's great gift to the world.

The lives of the French Impressionists, Renoir's older and younger contemporaries, lend themselves all too easily to romantic biography. Names like Manet, Pissarro, Monet, and Sisley conjure up the Paris of artists and literati described by Murger in his famous *Vie de Bohème*, the Paris of small cafés and bars, of countless art dealers and booksellers, the Paris of attic studios surrounded by a forest of black chimney-pots with their creaking cowls. All the misery and ecstasy, all the poverty and glory of the artist's life was realized in the lives of that generation of painters. They sounded all the material and intellectual heights and depths, and took possession of the world with tremendous vitality; their world was the present. In a passionate reaction against the now impotent historicity of 19th century art the Impressionists took a decisive step towards the problems of the day. Historical themes and historical costumes disappeared from their pictures, and the obligatory pilgrimages of artists to the home of antique art were a thing of the past.

The watchword was contemporaneousness — *être de son temps* — in the true sense of the word. The only things worthy of representation in painting are those things that happen, and are seen, today. That is the spirit of Impressionism. This assertion allowed of variation: one group — Boudin, Pissarro, Sisley — concerned themselves with landscape as being absolutely unhistorical and always modern; others, like Degas, studied the physiognomy and gestures of the people of their time and tried to create valid symbols for them; Manet invented a new style, flat, unceremonious, loud, which consciously contrasted with the dignified representation of important events in the painting of the past. Modernness was the passion, *contemporanéité* was the rational ground for existence. One lived in Paris without being domiciled there, was social without social ambitions, enjoyed the moment today, without granting it a sentimental thought tomorrow. Only a few could resist the attraction of this way of life: Cézanne, for example, whose modest income enabled him to lead an outwardly calm bourgeois existence. Renoir, however, who had decided to take up painting in Paris at the age of twenty-one although he was without any real means, would have been just the type for the Bohemian life of Paris if his character and origin had not endowed him with powers to protect him from unconditional fanatical concentration on the present. In order to understand those powers, it is necessary to go back to his earliest youth, even to his birth.

It is very tempting to place significance on the fact that it happened to be the town of Limoges where Pierre-Auguste Renoir was born on February 25, 1841: the town where, towards the end of the 15th century, art enamel was first produced and handed down from father to son in several artists' families till the end of the 17th century. It really seems as if the spirit of one of the great Limoges enamel painters had instilled into the child his love of bright, shining colours, his delicate taste, and his feeling for craftsmanship. But it was not only a case of the influence of the genius loci, for Renoir gained a thorough knowledge in the use of colours, and above all a love of good and lasting craftsmanship in five years of work in a Paris workshop for porcelain

Young Girl with Rose, 1886
Pastel. Collection of Durand-Ruel, Paris

painting. The boy had to start work at the age of ten, as his father, a small tailor from Limoges, had moved with his family to Paris in the vain hope of finding a better living there. Pierre-Auguste had to help to support the family, and the beginning in the porcelain workshop was very promising. The work soon gave him a light touch and a sure eye for the selection and combination of colours. Soon he had progressed from decorative to figurative work, and his repertoire ran from floral patterns to the portrait of Marie Antoinette, for which he was paid forty centimes apiece. The colours with which he mainly worked were those of the rococo period: delicate pinks, brilliant blues, and chrome yellow, on the gleaming white kaolin background. This trio of colours occurs again and again in his later pictures, where they are supplemented by many shades of green, violet, and a brilliant, fatty black. Those five years were happy ones for him, but came to an end through the invention of a system of printing on porcelain, which ousted the handworker in favour of a mechanical process. Renoir joined the workshop of a fan painter; here he painted scenes of gallantry after Boucher, Watteau, and Lancret. Later he painted curtains and decorations for mobile mission altars. The young journeyman was soon superior to his fellow-workers and the master, and was called a « baby Rubens » because of the astonishing bravura with which he handled colour.

His later development into a great artist, however, was decisively influenced by his early range of motifs as well as by his foundation of craftsmanship. Rococo pastoral scenes like « Embarkation to Cythera » by Watteau were always in demand, and Renoir had to provide them. So he spent his little free time in the Louvre where he diligently studied the composition of the French painters of the 18th century, their colours and their virtuoso brush technique.

He fell in love with the spirit of that period, and its elegance and lightness inspired his brush. It permeates his later works, despite the manifold influences of Courbet, Delacroix, and Ingres, like a tender melody, only occasionally obscured by the noises of the present.

Although his work for the missions promised to be very successful financially, and would have guaranteed him a modest career as an arts and crafts worker, he gave notice to his employer. He had saved enough money to be able to visit painting and drawing courses at the Ecole des Beaux-Arts. At the same time he joined the Gleyre Studio. Like most of the teachers who had their own schools, Gleyre's connection with the Ecole, the stronghold of the austere academic art, was very vague, and he was known among students of painting for his generosity and his artistic tolerance. Himself only a mediocre historical painter, his greatest importance lies in the fact that he taught the young generation the fundamental technical craftsmanship of painting without forcing their talent to conform to the Procrustes bed of traditional style. Renoir and his thirty or forty fellow students drew diligently from the nude at Gleyre's, one week the model was male, the next female; twice a week Gleyre went to the studio and corrected the perspective, the anatomy, the plastic effect of the body, and the colour. It was on such an occasion, when he was standing, no doubt a little nonplussed, in front of one of Renoir's daringly coloured pictures, that he disapprovingly asked if the pupil was painting for enjoyment. When Renoir innocently answered in the affirmative, — « if I didn't enjoy it I shouldn't do it » —, Gleyre was no little astonished, because nobody had ever yet painted there for fun. However boisterous and Bohemian the activities may have been in all the painting classes of the Ecole while the teacher's back was turned, painting was a deadly serious thing for the young artists. They saw their careers in their various stages stretching out quite clearcut in front of them; the annual exams, competition for the *Prix de Rome*, the scholarships, the acceptance of their pictures for the annual Autumn Exhibitions, and finally the commissioning of works by the state. In the distance beckoned the honour of being made a *Chevalier de la Légion d'Honneur* and a member of the Academy. But Renoir painted because he enjoyed it.

There was also one other student who was a source of considerable difficulty for Gleyre. It was Monet, who, in Le Havre, where he had spent his youth, had already « arrived » as a caricaturist. Gleyre disapproved of his pictures, too, because the young man reproduced the models with merciless accuracy just as they were — with too large feet, with a short, thick-set body, or with a thick skull. Gleyre criticized him and instructed him to reproduce the model in an idealized form according to the then valid classical canons of beauty. If in Renoir's daring use of colour the dangerous influence of Delacroix was suspected, the Delacroix, who was already poisoning the youngest students and alienating them from the principle that the line was the only valid medium of artistic expression, in Monet the academicians saw the realism of Courbet, who must have appeared to them to be no less corrupting. The corrections made by these teachers of the Ecole were like somebody hastily papering over the cracks in the wall of a house in the hope of thus saving the whole structure from ruin while decay was already taking its irresistible course in the foundations.

There were in fact signs of crisis in the Ecole des Beaux-Arts and the whole of its official art; everybody felt it, supporters and enemies. Renoir and Monet quickly became known among the Gleyre students as revolutionaries, although they, unlike the others, sat quietly and diligently behind their easels: at that time it was considered much more reprehensible to apply a certain burning red to the canvas than, for example, to throw dripping paint brushes at the model when the teacher was absent.

The beginning of the crisis in academic painting, glaringly obvious by the time Renoir, Monet, Bazille and Sisley were attending the Gleyre studio and the Ecole, can be traced back to the year 1855, when a comprehensive international art exhibition, in which the French section

THE UMBRELLAS, about 1883; 71″ × 59″, National Gallery, London

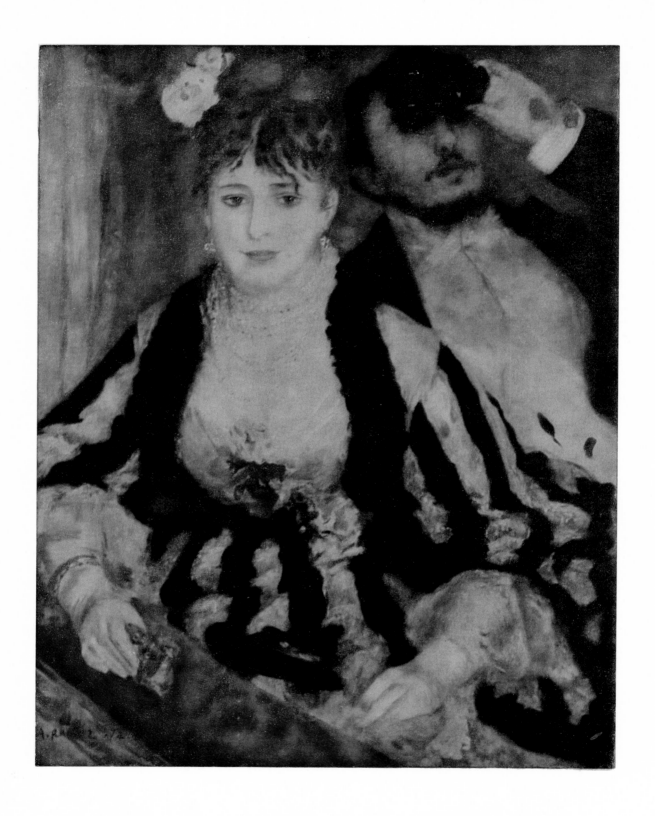

THE LOGE, 1874; 32″ × 25″, Courtauld Collection, Tate Gallery, London

THE FIRST EVENING OUT, about 1876; 26″ × 20″, Tate Gallery, London

LADY WITH VEIL, 1880; 24″ × 20″, Louvre, Paris

PORTRAIT OF THÉRÈSE BÉRARD, 1879; 22″ × 19″
Private Collection, New York (formerly Collection of Mrs. Thurneyssen, Paris)

Young Girl.   Albertina, Vienna

took up most space, was assembled in Paris for the great World's Fair.   At that time one painter already dared to rebel against the artistic dictatorship of the almighty director of the Académie des Beaux-Arts, Count Nieuwekerke, and he opened an exhibition of his rejected pictures near the exhibition building: it was Courbet.   His *Pavillon du Réalisme* was the opening shot in the battle.   Delacroix was driven into the opposition's camp at the same time, for, although a large number of his pictures were exhibited, the majority of the medals and prizes went to Ingres and his supporters.   Thus the artists were split into two camps, which fought one another with brush and pen, in the press and in public meetings, with intrigues and physical force.   The battle cries were « Hurrah for classical idealism, » « Hurrah for realism », « Hurrah for line, Hurrah for colour. »   Ingres, the members of the Académie and the teachers of the Ecole on the one side, Delacroix, Courbet, and the painters of the Barbizon school on the other.   An unequal battle, if one considers the outward positions of power.   Behind Ingres stood the Académie des Beaux-Arts, as one of the departments of the Institut de France: the patron, but also the absolute ruler of the arts and sciences.   The influence of the Académie extended to the Ecole des Beaux-Arts whose teachers were elected by it; in addition, the juries in charge of admission of works to the exhibitions and the distributions of prizes were under its authority.   Finally the Académie had the decisive word concerning purchases by museums and the official commissioning of artists.   As the public accepted the judgment of the institution without reservation an artist outlawed by the Académie was as good as non-existent; he had no chance of even exhibiting his works.

Edmond Renoir at Menton, 1883
Ink and Crayon. Collection of P. Rosenberg

Renoir and his friends at Gleyre's took no part in these battles or in the preparations for the Autumn Exhibition in 1862. They themselves could not yet think of submitting anything for the exhibition, but they watched the hectic activity of their older colleagues: press opinion was bought, individual members of the jury were waited on, the hanging committee was bribed so that the pictures which were finally accepted were also advantageously placed. The business of art devoured everyone's energy, and social reputation was more important than artistic quality. A further symptom of the decrepitude of the official art institutions was the sudden influx of students to the studio of the heretic Courbet, in which models were painted realistically. The academic training bored the art students, and so they sought for new stimuli. On the other hand the jury applied even stricter standards for the current exhibition than before — after they had first protected themselves against blunders by abandoning the system of anonymous entry. It could no longer happen that anonymous works by the most important members of the Académie were rejected. That was the situation before the Autumn Exhibition of 1863, which was the immediate cause of the outbreak of the battle. This time Renoir had also submitted a picture, a female nude reclining on a divan, with a dwarf next to her playing a guitar — an absolutely academic motif, painted, as far as one can judge from contemporary reports, in dark academic colours.

When it became known that the jury had this time rejected more than four thousand works, there was a revolt of the painters who had had their works rejected; many of them had been represented in previous exhibitions. Among them were Jongkind and Manet, who, with his *Spanish Guitarist* had already enjoyed great success. Renoir's picture was of course also rejected.

The general indignation came to the ears of Emperor Napoleon III, and since, for reasons of prestige, he could no longer cancel the decision of the official jury, he gave the sensational order for the establishment of the *Salon des Refusés*, which gave every artist the chance of exhibiting or withdrawing his rejected works. Many wisely withdrew so as to avoid the jury's anger on later occasions. The avant-garde, including Whistler, Fantin-Latour, Pissarro, and Cézanne, exhibited, of course. Perhaps the artists had hoped that the public would declare for them, and that the jury would have to be dismissed. In that, however, they had deceived themselves, for the masses demanded their heroic scenes and their genre pictures, meticulously painted, and their still lifes with naturalistic apples to make their mouths water, and noble nude studies of similar effect. For example, a leg in the foreground would have to be executed down to the smallest detail, contours were not allowed to swim, and objects in the background had to appear darker. The public made fun of the *Salon des Refusés*, while the press split into two camps. Zola discovered an intellectual affinity in this opposition, this revolutionary

18

spirit, and he greeted the exhibition and its artists with enthusiasm, many of them were, after all, his friends. The critic and writer Zacharie Astruc took a similar attitude. The official art critics, on the other hand, spewed hatred and irony. It is true that the public was amused by the battles, but at least its attention was drawn to the abuses in the art world; the Académie finally found itself forced basically to reorganise itself. But it was too late; the students changed to other schools, and above all the Louvre was filled with copyists who believed that they could learn more from the old masters than from the traditional school. Gleyre's studio was also deserted, and closed in 1864. Thus the friends Renoir, Monet, Bazille, and Sisley were thrown onto their own resources.

Now Monet, who was older and more experienced than the others, became the driving force. He had once before painted on the French Atlantic coast near Le Havre with Boudin and Jongkind. After the Gleyre studio shut down he set up his easel once more in the open air. He took his friends with him, and painted in the Fontainebleau Woods near Chailly. The industrious Renoir, who was always so ready to learn, by no means approved of the turn things

Couple on a Slope, 1883. Pencil

had taken because he had enjoyed studying at Gleyre's; he could not know that a meeting of decisive importance for him would take place in the Fontainebleau Woods. Diaz, who belonged to the group of painters who had settled in nearby Barbizon and changed from historical scenes to landscapes, watched Renoir at work and criticized his frequent use of dark colours. He instructed Renoir in the constant and exact observation of nature and opened his eyes to the endless variety of nuances and shades of colour which could be found, for example, on the ground in a wood. This meeting spelled Renoir's liberation from those dark tones which gave the works of all the academic painters of that period the appearance of old, smoke-darkened antiques.

Nevertheless Renoir's generation's most important discoveries lay not so much in the realm of colour as in that of content. In this field Courbet was still the ideal. Renoir emulated him, and painted works even in his later years that recall the brutal realism of that artist; and as long as he took over Courbet's subjects he used Courbet's dark tones. Another ideal was the notorious Manet, who had dared, in his picture *Le Déjeuner sur l'herbe*, taking up an idea in one of Giorgione's pictures, to show a nude woman next to two men in modern, fashionable clothes. What was permitted for an Italian at the turn of the 15th century was considered indecent in Manet. So Renoir also painted a realistic picture in which he depicted his friends in the Cabaret de la Mère Anthony, smoking and chatting, with the pretty and reputedly wanton host's daughter clearing the table, and, between scribblings on a wall in the background a charcoal caricature of Murger. This harmless genre piece, already painted, by the way, with an enchanting softness and with a strong plastic quality, was nevertheless far removed from Manet's vigorous and audacious actuality. On another occasion Renoir tried to emulate Courbet's techni-

Pencil Study for the Portrait of Julie Manet, 1887; Private Collection, Paris

que, in that he applied his paint with a spatula instead of with a brush. The surface of a woodland scene near Fontainebleau with his friend Lecoeur thus took on a coarse structure, as though thick oil paint had been applied to rough masonry. This technique, however, was not consistent with his artistic ideals, which were already calling for a more delicate and subtle use of colour. But he continued to experiment, although every now and again, since he found it difficult to burn his boats so uncompromisingly as Monet did for example, he would produce a picture completely academic in content and form. No doubt Renoir kept one eye on the Exhibition, and his pictures in the academic manner may have been painted with a view to securing an acceptance for the Autumn Exhibition. It is a fact that his *Esmeralda*, painted in the academic style, depicting the beautiful gipsy woman of Victor Hugo's *Notre Dame de Paris* dancing in the Place de Grève, was accepted in 1864. But this success did not give him undiluted pleasure; it may even have seemed to him somewhat dishonest, for although he had not become a fanatical follower of plein-airism — painting in the open air in natural light — the dark « academic sauce » had been distasteful to him ever since his meeting with Diaz. There-

20

fore he destroyed the picture soon afterwards. In 1865, however, two pictures, which, remembering Diaz's advice he had painted directly from nature, were accepted.

His period of experimentation lasted until the outbreak of war in 1870. But that period produced two famous works which were important to his artistic development. One of them is the *Lise with the Parasol* (1867). Here, for the first time, he carries his idea of coloured shadows to its logical conclusion. The delicate, blossom-white dress of the girl is painted with infinite love, weightless, it seems not to have been applied with the brush, but to have been breathed on to the canvas. Blue and violet shadows play on it, and on the white hat there are reflections from the green foliage. Renoir's brush technique in the tradition of the old masters; the colours are carefully and smoothly applied, so that there are no individual brush strokes to be seen.

Only two years later, however, in the picture *La Grenouillière*, Renoir managed to free himself completely of the past also in the technical sense: the picture shows a few boats on the water, a colourful gathering on a small island, and a wooded bank in the background. To give the spectator an impression of the reflections dancing on the wavelets, reflections which here have formed a bizarre image of the people and things on the bank, and there have been dispersed by a breath of wind into small patches of dark and light, Renoir uses clearly defined brush strokes. If one placed any value on dating a phenomenon of painting technique — in this case the brush stroke characteristic of Impressionism — one could do it here, for in this picture

of Renoir's, and in that of his friend Monet, who painted the same subject at the same time, appear for the first time small patches of colour, which, at a certain distance, give the spectator the complex impression of a blue-green pattern of wavelets.

Such discoveries were always sensational for the young painters, who passed paintings around among themselves, and vigorously discussed quality and technique. Before the Franco-German War, which interrupted work and social life for a time, the meeting place was either near Paris on the Grenouillière (« frog pond ») in Père Fournaises's restaurant in Bougival, which had become Monet's and Renoir's haunt, or in Paris itself in the Quartier Batignolles. Here the Café Guerbois was the Impressionists' meeting place. Apart from Renoir, Monet, Sisley, and Bazille, Manet also occasionally put in an appearance; although he did not like to « fraternize » with the Bohemians because he had hopes of one day being recognized by the Académie, he never-

Woman with Child

theless felt very much at home in that circle of kindred spirits. Pissarro and Cézanne, and the caustic, intellectual Degas also belonged to the circle. Renoir himself felt completely at home among this group of friends. He laughed at the jokes though he was often bored by the heated arguments, for nothing was more foreign to him than theoretical discussions on art. He believed in experiment, not theory. Any kind of fanatical devotion to a particular idea, style, or technique, was also foreign to his nature. Even though he was dubbed a revolutionary at the Ecole, he was an « unwilling » revolutionary; he certainly did not want to arouse the world, or bring new truths to light: he quite simply wanted to give pleasure with his pictures. The *épater le bourgeois* was not in tune with his optimistic, philanthropic being. A feeling for the relationship between artist and public had remained more vital in him than in any other Impressionist, indeed, perhaps he was the only one in whom it survived at all. That was someting he had learned in his youth when he had had to work to order as a craftsman in direct contact with the customer: the term *l'art pour l'art* has no place in craftsmanship, and as Renoir painted his pictures with the same joy of creation as he had decorated his porcelain, fans, and curtains, art for art's sake had no place in his painting either. For Renoir, then, it was not a question of conscience whether one should make compromises or not in order to get a picture into an exhibition; for him it was at most a question of whether or not he was gradually becoming bored by the academic style.

That Renoir could not join his friends in their modern outlook which demanded the glorification of the moment is now understandable. Life and art were for Renoir one and the same thing, nourished from the same source, and if one can compare the other artists to candles which quickly burn out, then one can compare Renoir to a plant which slowly but surely develops, always turning its blossoms towards the sun throughout the long summer, bears rich fruit, and withers.

The circle of painters in the Café Guerbois, which had been scattered by the war, met again after the end of the Commune of 1871 and threw themselves into their work with enthusiasm, unperturbed by the sometimes desperate situation. Renoir had spent the war months comparatively quietly as a Curassier in a regiment in Marseille. The portraits of his captain, Darras, and his wife are from this period. They are brilliantly painted, but they lack the atmosphere which one can feel, for example, in the earlier portrait of Sisley. It is true that the contours are still harder there than in the Darras portraits, the colours harder and dryer. But that cannot disguise the fact that the spirit of Sisley fills the picture from frame to frame in an indefinable fashion; the background is alive, and there is not merely a model in the clothes, but a personality. *Captain Darras* was painted by Renoir to commission as a show piece with the whole of his technical ability. There was, however, no inner relationship with this man and his world, and so he could not incorporate it in his picture.

Monet, who had fled to England during the war, now took over the leadership of the group again, which, to begin with, was more of an artistic unity than an organized one. In 1872 he had rented a house in Argenteuil near Paris on the banks of the Seine in order to be able to live with his beloved motifs – water, sailing and rowing boats, woods and meadows. Renoir often visited him there at work. They sat next to one another with their easels, and together discovered ways of translating what they saw into light and colour. Gradually the figures and things in Renoir's works lost their clumsiness, and the heavy, earthy quality of some of his figures, taken over from Courbet and still traceable in his *Bather* of 1870, began to disappear. Renoir now freed himself from Courbet's influence, and turned to Delacroix as his ideal, but his dependence on his new hero is different, more subtle. Renoir has become surer, his colours are taking on a new independence, making it inevitable that he should turn to Delacroix. It is true that, but for the existence of a few pictures with oriental motifs, which, both in form and

Louis Valtat, about 1904; Lithograph

Claude Renoir, 1904; Lithograph

content, were consciously painted after Delacroix's works, it would be a difficult task to prove this influence simply on the strength of the landscapes and portraits. One would search vainly for Delacroix's wild, glowing colours in, for example, *The Loge* of 1874. Perhaps one could here point out the darkly glowing background, the combination of violet, gold, and black in the

WOMAN WITH PARASOL, 1877
18″ × 23″, Museum of Fine Arts, Boston (Collection of J. T. Spaulding)

WOMAN AT THE PIANO, 1875
37″ × 29″, Art Institute, Chicago
(Collection of Mr. and Mrs. Martin A. Ryerson)

PORTRAIT OF JEANNE SAMARY (Half-Length), 1877; 22″ × 18″, Museum of Occidental Art, Moscow

GONDOLA ON THE CANAL GRANDE, VENICE, 1881
21″ × 26″, Collection of Werner H. Kramarsky, New York

St. Mark's Square, Venice, 1881
25″ × 31″, Institute of Arts, Minneapolis, U.S.A. (formerly Pinakothek, Munich)

PORTRAIT OF CHOQUET, 1875; 18″ × 14″, Collection of O. Reinhart, Winterthur, Switzerland

PORTRAIT OF MLLE SAMARY, 1877; 32″ × 26″, Comédie Française, Paris

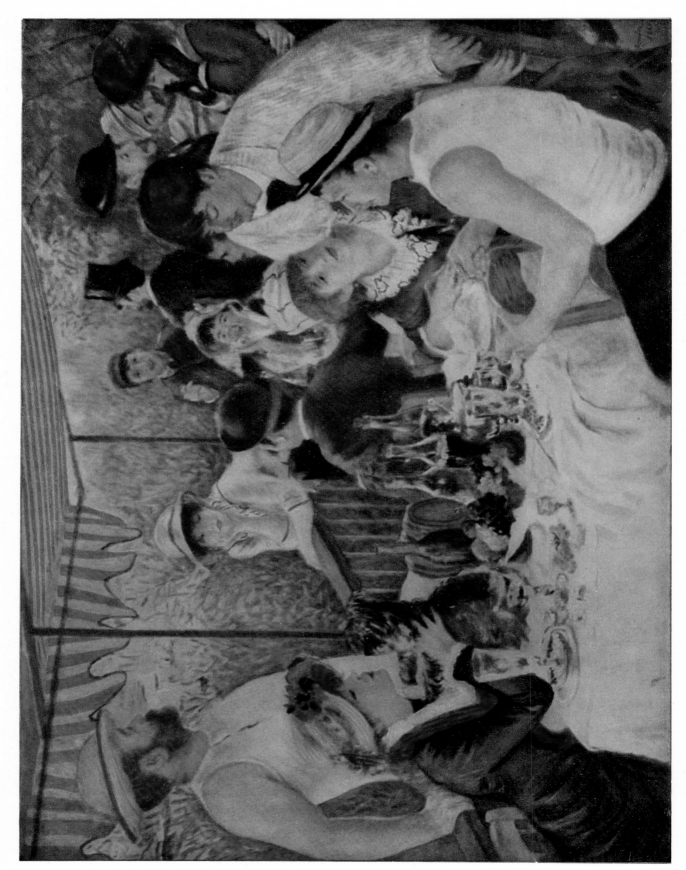

THE BOATING PARTY, 1881; 51″ × 68″, Phillips Memorial Gallery, Washington, D.C.

Peasant Woman with Cow and Sheep: Red Chalk

foreground, and compare them to Delacroix's oriental splendour of colour, and perhaps one could find something of Delacroix's interiors in the picture *Woman at the Piano*. The red patches on the sailing boats in the *Regatta at Argenteuil* could also have been taken from the palette of the older master. Here a piece of velvet and some gilded mouldings, there a glittering candle-holder on the piano, a coloured carpet; in another picture a few especially daring touches of colour where the influence of the painter of *Femmes d'Alger* is evident; the essence of what Renoir found in Delacroix, however, is so thoroughly assimilated that his hero is hardly more than a catalyst which has quickened up the process of development: the awakening of colour to a life of its own, to vibration. This process of development also brings with it a loosening up of contours. In accordance with the theory of marginal radiation, which was later to become part of the Impressionist colour theory, the contour is abandoned. The physical phenomenon, that two adjacent colours cannot be sharply distinguished from one another by the human eye because their radiation overlaps where they meet to form complementary colours, thus making the margins become undefined, is emphasized in the work of art. A comparison of *Portrait of Sisley* with the later *The Loge* clearly shows the development. The brilliant white of the necker-chief in the portrait is sharply separated from the dark jacket and the somewhat lighter waist-coat. Where are such contours on the couple in *The Loge?* The white shirt-front of the man, and his black evening dress, form a zone of transition which veils the margins of the two colour areas, and on the dress of the young woman black and white flicker, disperse, and merge into one another. Nevertheless they never mix to form a grey, because the brush always places small patches next to one another, without having previously mixed them on the palette: that is left to the eye of the spectator.

. What Renoir had for the first time done instinctively in the picture painted by the Gre-nouillière with coarse brush strokes now becomes a principle of composition. He logically reduces the brush strokes to a round comma shape, so that the flickering and vibration now cover the whole picture. This technique, which Monet used for many years, and Pissarro continued to use even right up to his last pictures, was finally perfected by Signac with the help of mathematical calculation, for Renoir it was only a stage of development. He always had command of many possible ways of representing colour and light, and used the particular technique that suited his artistic intention of the moment; thus he was continually finding new ways of representing the world in the medium of colour. With a daring which recalls the late Monet he unfolds over the Seine in the Argenteuil picture an atmospheric colour display beginning on the left with pinkish gold tones, in which here and there, and more often towards the middle, a blue appears: a dramatic battle between day and twilight takes place above the boats, whose sails — in colours ranging from harsh white to blue — join in. And the whole is intensified by the reflec-tion in the water. During the same period, however, Renoir painted other pictures with a pastel-like smoothness which recalls his training as a craftsman. A delicate glaze lies on the face of the woman in the *Loge*. The fleeting pink of the cheeks changes in soft transitional tones to the ivory glow of nose and forehead, with the sharply defined mouth below. Only the eyes are given soft contours, which lend the gaze a certain dewy quality. A similar mixture of techniques can be found in *Les Grands Boulevards*. Here, however, there are no meticulously painted details; everything vibrates and flickers in that mild light of Paris so fascinating to painters. The moistness of the air lends the colours a special intensity, never making them harsh and loud, however, for the softly blue sky mutes them to a mat glow. This blue sky is painted very thickly in Renoir's picture compared to the green of the trees. *Les Grands Boulevards!* — that is a landscape after Renoir's own heart. An exciting feast for the intellect and the senses. A moist breath of air drifts across from the Seine, and mixes with the dust of the streets and the scent and tobacco smoke of the parading ladies and gentlemen. Here

First Sketch for the Sculpture « Venus ».   Pencil

and there the sound of a laugh, a child's voice, rises above the surging crowds, against the background sound of horses' hooves and elegant carriages.

The decade between the end of the war in 1871 and the year 1882, when the Impressionists exhibited for the last time as a group in the Exposition des Indépendants, was for Renoir a time of development from careful groping to an obvious ne plus ultra of volatilization of form and activation of colour via increasing control of the means of expression, and even their occasional routine application. During this decade Renoir and his friends lived in close intellectual and social community with a group of revolutionary artists whose central figure was Manet. Manet, though by no means an Impressionist of the first water, dominated by his personality. His sparkling charm, the brilliance of his argumentation, combined with a somewhat dandyish snobbishness, which he consciously cultivated to maintain the distance between himself and his inferiors, predestined him to be the leader, or, to put it more accurately, spokesman of the group. Manet had given up his haunt, The Café Bade, before the war, and now frequented the Café Guerbois, which still exists today in the Avenue de Clichy as Brasserie Muller. In the evening discussions — and what else could the painters do after dusk except meet for discussion, since in the age of petroleum lamps it was not possible to work after nightfall — in these discussions the themes were plein-airism, the admission to exhibitions, the importance or lack of importance of the old masters for contemporary art, cultural politics, the great importance of Delacroix, and the debatable position of Courbet. One can imagine the fervour of these discussions, in which men of such different temperament and intellect took part. There were Manet and Degas, the one witty, the other caustic. Pissarro, a radical socialist and convinced atheist with the courage of his principles, but nevertheless of great kindness and always ready to help others. A rare guest was Cézanne; noncommittal, taciturn, he expressed his opinions with vehemence and could not bear to be contradicted. Apart from the painters Braquemond, Fantin-Latour, Guillemet, Constantin Guys, Monet, and Sisley, the writers Duranty, Zola, and Duret, and the photographer Nadar were frequently present; it was in Nadar's studio on the Boulevard des Capucines where the first memorable Impressionist exhibition took place in 1874.

There many descriptions of the people and happenings of this decisive decade were provided by the authors of contemporary letters and documents. There are also interesting descriptions of Renoir who, when he did not happen to be visiting his friend Monet in Argenteuil, or his parents in Louveciennes, or, towards the end of the seventies his friend and patron Bérard on his estate in Normandy, was a frequent guest at the Café Guerbois. Like many of his friends he had never had the opportunity for an education such as Manet or Degas had had, and it was therefore difficult for him to join in the discussion with water-tight arguments; apart from that it was difficult for him, a thoroughly untheoretical person, to see why, for example, Zola was so annoyed by the nymphs in Corot's woodland pictures, and wanted to see peasant women in their place. It was sufficient for him if they were well painted. Renoir, slim, mobile, and modest, was, despite his poverty, of an irresistible gaiety. He was unashamed of his Parisian dialect, and was prepared to laugh at any joke, even if it was not as intellectual as those of Degas. For him life was full of joy and beauty, and he was daily enchanted with it. He could not understand why one should worry oneself with serious theoretical discussions about the past, present, or future. This optimism of his was severely tested again and again. He had to fight against the indifference or disregard of the public, the brusque refusal from the official institutions, and an often bitter poverty. But he was not alone in this battle; however much his comrades may have differed in their ideas, they were united in their determination to open up new paths for painting whatever the opposition. Out of this desire was born the idea of arranging, at their own expense, an exhibition which should include for the first time works by artists who were pursuing new artistic aims. Thus, on April 15th 1874, an exhibition of

36

Orange Seller, 1885-90; Red Chalk

pictures by Cézanne, Renoir, Degas, Guillaumin, Monet, Berthe Morisot, Pissarro, and Sisley, was opened in Nadar's, the photographer's studio. Among other works, Renoir exhibited his « Box » and « Dances ». It was an ironic touch of fate that this very exhibition should have given a name to the whole movement. Monet exhibited a picture which he had painted in Le Havre, called *Impression, Soleil levant*. The critic Louis Leroy picked out the first word for the title of his article in Charivari, *Exposition des Impressionistes*, and thus the group was named. The venture turned out to be a scandal as well as a commercial failure. Renoir came in for less calumny than the others owing to his « tamer » pictures. The rage of the public was vented mainly on Cézanne and Monet. Phrases like « ludicrous collection of absurdities », and « painters who have declared war on beauty » were used in the criticisms, and the story went round that the Impressionists painted by filling a pistol with paint and then shooting blindly at the canvas. There is a touch of tragi-comedy about the fact that hardly a hundred years later, a certain section of the public, though surrounding itself with reproductions of Impressionist works, and smiling disdainfully at the ignorance of the public of that time, uses similar foolish comparisons about its own contemporary painting.

Discouraged for further communal undertakings by the failure of both this exhibition and the auction in the Hotel Drouot in the following year, Renoir tried hard to secure more portrait commissions. The stubborn idealism of a Monet or Cézanne were foreign to him. He was prepared to compromise and paint the kind of works that his clients wanted. A story Ambroise Vollard had from Renoir illustrates this point: « And the trouble I had to get the money, whenever I did by chance get a paid commission! I can remember the time, for example, when I painted a portrait of a bootmaker's wife, for a pair of boots. Every time I thought I had finished and began to think hopefully of my boots, an aunt, or daughter, or even a house-maid, would come in: 'Don't you think that my niece, my mother, the Mistress, has a much shorter nose than that?' I wanted my boots, and gave the shoemaker's wife a nose like Madame de Pompadour's. »

During the years 1874-75 Renoir was given strong moral and financial support by the art dealer Durand-Ruel, who, with courage and a sure instinct, gambled on the Impressionists by buying their pictures for a long period without at first being able to sell any at all, by Caillebotte, a well-to-do private person and ship's engineer, who painted for pleasure and bought pictures — mainly those « unsaleable » pictures of his friends, and by Choquet, a civil servant who spent his not very large income on works by Cézanne and Renoir. In 1876 this circle of patrons and friends was joined by Charpentier, the publisher of the journal « La Vie Moderne », and later by the industrialist Paul Bérard. Among other things, Renoir received from all of them, countless portrait commissions which saved him from the extremes of poverty. Many of the portraits from this period are still painted with great caution, one can sense the trouble that the painter took to achieve physical resemblance. Despite this, the portraits of young Rivière, an avant-garde writer, and Choquet, the white-haired art-lover and collector, are extremely lively. Intelligence, sparkling esprit, and nervous sensibility play about the mouth and eyes of Choquet; his hand is touching his chin, but only, it seems, for a moment, then it will break into restless movement again. The muted colours, blue-white and greenish tones dominating, give the picture a certain solemnity; but above all one senses a fascinating discrepancy between this man with his eloquent eyes and the impersonal, conventional background. The brush technique in the « Portrait of Rivière », carried out in restless small commas and strokes, is much livelier. The intellectual courage, recklessness, and excitability of the young writer are reflected in every form and every colour. Conventional taste also plays a part here in the way the head is turned into profile position, which, in a certain sense, reduces the physiognomy to a symbol, and in the green background. Again the personality of the sitter seems to rebel

Nanny with Child, 1902

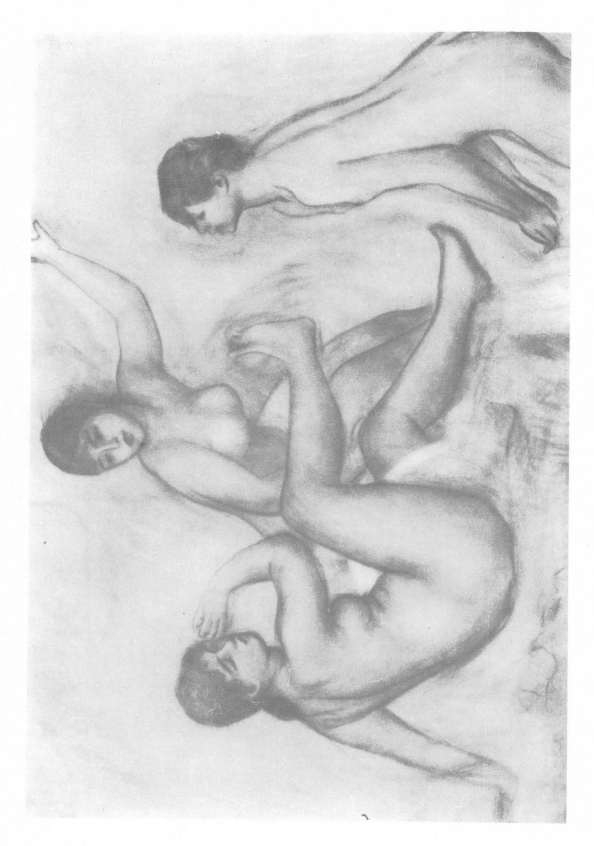

Women Bathing 1884-85; Red Chalk. Private Collection, Paris

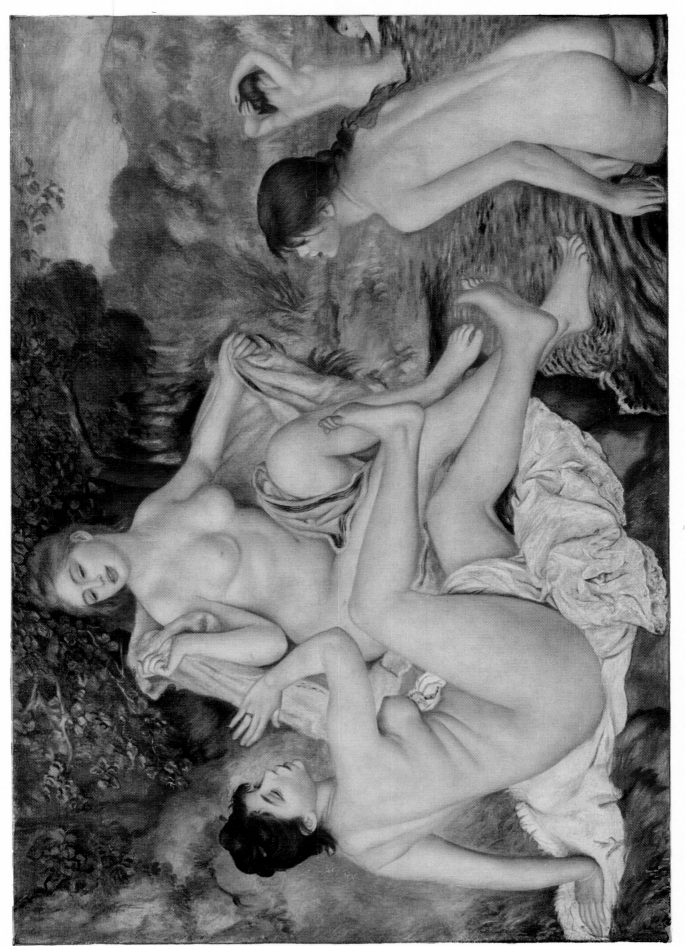

WOMEN BATHING (GRANDES BAIGNEUSES), 1883-85; 45" × 28", Collection of Caroll S. Tyson, Philadelphia

L'Estaque, 1882; 26″ × 32″, Museum of Fine Arts, Boston

42

A TERRACE IN CAGNES, 1905
The Ishibashi Collection, Tokyo

◁

CHURCH AT CAGNES, 1905
16″ × 13″, Collection of Durand-Ruel, Paris

DANCE IN THE TOWN
1883; 71″ × 36″
Collection of Durand-Ruel
Paris

DANCE AT BOUGIVAL
1883; 71″ × 36″
Museum of Fine Arts
Boston

Study for
« Dance at Bougival »,
1883, Ink and Crayon
Collection of P. Rosenberg

◁

LA COIFFURE
1888; 32″ × 23″,
Collection of Durand-Ruel, Paris

against the severity of the form. Such a refined form of painting, with its most subtle spiritual values as can be found in these two pictures, particularly in that of Choquet, can, however, no longer be described. The 18th century, with its unique art of portraiture, manifested brilliantly in the miniatures alone, is behind this picture. There have been, perhaps, more powerful portraits, those of Düerer, El Greco, Rembrandt, and Goya, for example, where the person represented casts a spell over the spectator, crushes him with the strength of his personality, overwhelms or fascinates. But there can scarcely be another portrait painted with so little pretentiousness as that of Choquet, whose goodness, intelligence, and urbanity touch us afresh every time we look at it.

Jeanne Samary, too, a young, very beautiful Parisian actress, who was a frequent visitor to Renoir's roomy studio in the rue St. Georges, sat for two pictures, a full-length and a half-length portrait. Now the final step to a thorough-going Impressionist technique is taken in the portrait, as it has already been taken in landscape. The unmixed colours are applied thickly, blue and green in small strokes and points, irregularly placed on the décolleté dress; a couple of dabs of colour represent the stones in the gold bracelet. In the upper half of the picture the colours seem to be moving, the red of the background creates the impression of a boiling liquid, on the right darker scraps are drawn into the vortex. This movement has also taken possession of the coppery gold hair. Individual strands flicker outwards from the centre like the protruberances of a fiery star, surrounding the face with an aura. Towards the middle the forms and colours consolidate, the red of the mouth and the blue of the eyes are like a crystallization of the turmoil of colours surrounding them. The colour structure also calls for musical comparisons. One is reminded of theme and variations, of Wagner's *Leitmotive*. Indeed, such comparisons have a certain validity, for Renoir was deeply interested in music. Charles Gounod, Renoir's music teacher, was the first to awaken the boy's interest, and this interest was kept alive in later life by his friendship with the musician Chabrier, and with Faure, the baritone of the Paris Opera, and finally by his enthusiasm for Wagner's music, which was acclaimed by the Impressionists mainly for the way it broke with traditional forms.

Here, too, as in the Choquet portrait, the personality is given a façade in keeping with conventionalism; the pose and the full-face position with its uninhibited, coquettish gaze, attributes of the actress, and a certain importunity of the colours, belong to the theatrical world.

In these works Renoir takes his first steps in the dangerous career of the fashionable portraitist. The commissions secured for him by his patrons and friends poured in. Renoir was en vogue. The publisher Charpentier, who commissioned portraits of his wife and children from Renoir, introduced him, who had so far but rarely ventured into socially higher circles than that of the small circle of his painter friends, to the world of the intellectuals in Paris. Zola, Edmond de Goncourt, Flaubert, Daudet, Maupassant, and Turgenjev were regular guests in Madame Charpentier's salon. It was inevitable that the sensitive painter should now also capture this mondaine world in his pictures. A typical example of this is the family portrait *Mme. Charpentier and Her Children*. The effect, with the formal pose of the woman and the two small girls in the luxurious salon, is very conventional and mondaine. The wonderful sheen of the silky materials, and the charming faces of the children, however, give the picture the same artistic quality as distinguishes the portrait of Samary, and which always lends his pictures a quality of timelessness. The only really Impressionist feature of this family portrait is the still life in the background: the table set with flowers, fruit, and glasses in front of the red wallpaper and the colourful curtain; only here was Renoir's artistic temperament given full rein, and, just as if he was once more invoking Delacroix, he succeeded in combining splendour with sparkling colour, as a contrast to the smooth beauty of the painted materials in the foreground.

Washerwoman and Studies for a Portrait, 1890-95
Red Chalk.   Collection of P. Rosenberg

Head of a Girl

As he expected, this family portrait and the portrait of Samary ensured his acceptance into the Salon of 1879, if perhaps more by reason of the famous subjects than of the artistic qualities. But still, he did receive 1,000 francs for the family portrait — a princely sum, if one considers the fact that many painters in those days had to be content if they could get a hundred francs for a picture.

Ever since the first Impressionist Exhibition in Boulevard des Capucines and the unsuccessful Vente Drouot, the Impressionists had had to fight hard against the indifference of the public and violent attacks in the press in order to maintain not only their artistic, but also their material existence. It was a battle of life and death in the truest sense of the word. Sisley died in utter poverty and despair, and Monet attempted to commit suicide. In their extreme distress the painters formed into a close community. They helped one another selflessly by introducing one another to art dealers and collectors. In 1873 Renoir was introduced by his friends to Durand-Ruel, who immediately bought a few of his pictures, and through Degas he

Ambroise Vollard, 1904; Lithograph

met Duret, one of the few art critics who had already unconditionally declared for the Impressionists. In Argenteuil Monet had made friends with Caillebotte, the owner of the neighbouring estate, and immediately introduced Renoir to him. Soon Caillebotte included Renoir in his friendship, and bought his pictures also. Renoir, for his part, had hardly been given a commission by Choquet, when he took him to Père Tanguy's paint shop, to show him Cézanne's pictures. Cézanne then took Choquet to Monet's studio. It is known that even Manet hung his friends' pictures in his own studio when he was expecting a visit by a well-to-do collector. On the other hand there were bitter fights within the group concerning who should be invited to take part in the Impressionist Exhibition and who should not. In 1877, for the third Exhibition of the group, all the Impressionists were represented together for the last time: Cézanne, Renoir, Degas, Monet, Morisot, Pissarro, Sisley; but from then on the group gradually disintegrated. Renoir began to be given recognition by the Salon, and after 1877 only took part once more in the Impressionist Exhibitions: in 1882. But by that time he no longer really belonged; he had given up plein-airism, and his journey to Italy in the previous year had prepared the way for a new phase in his work.

The five years before that, however, had brought forth the first great harvest. Some readers have perhaps followed with a certain impatience Renoir's cautious approach to the Impressionist technique in the beginning. Already his *Lise* raised hopes that the liberation of colour was imminent, and these hopes were fulfilled in a few pictures, among them the *Regatta at Argenteuil;* at the same time, however, his development appeared to be retarded in the series of impressive portraits, which to a certain extent represented his « official » production. It was only after the year 1876 that all the works which we count among the masterpieces of Impressionism were produced: *The Swing* (1876), *Le Moulin de la Galette* (1877), *The First Evening Out* (circa 1875),

Girl at Her Toilet; Red Chalk

54

The Boating Party (1881). It is possible to select a whole series of masterpieces from Renoir's works without including a landscape — something that would be impossible with any of the other Impressionists; for Renoir's optical susceptibility is directly dependent on people, or, more precisely, on women and girls, and the feminine element becomes stronger and stronger in his later works. The two friends on the bench in the Moulin de la Gallette are not only the formal, but also the spiritual centre of the picture. And if one glances from there towards the dancing couples, one's eyes come to rest on the young girl in the left foreground, gracefully leaning against her partner. Bright laughter seems to mix with the sound of music drifting across the scene, and the warm sunlight, casting bright patches on the gay company, lends radiance to the Sunday dresses of the women, their hair, and their faces. The people created by Renoir are always filled with a warm joy of being; this emotion forms a part of the tense expectancy of the young girl in the picture *The First Evening Out,* and of the playful flirtatiousness of the company of rowers.

The Fêtes Champétres of the 18th century, with their dances, swings, and picnics are recreated here in a different guise; less refined, more bourgeois, more robust, but full of urgency, and, through the feasts of colour, heightened to feasts of life.

Cancelled Feasts was what Meier-Graefe called Renoir's phase of development between 1881 and the turn of the century, a very apt term which justly characterizes what was happening in Renoir's painting at that time. His contemporaries also had the same feeling about it, they were disappointed that the splendid series of sensual and colourful Impressionistic feasts, from *Lise, La Moulin de la Galette, Jeanne Samary,* to *The Boating Party* had come to an end.

Girl with Basket

Woman Drying Herself; Pen and Ink Drawing. Louvre, Paris

SLEEPING BAIGNEUSE, 1897; 32″ × 25″
Collection of O. Reinhart, Winterthur, Switzerland

BATHING WOMEN, 1916; 15″ × 19″, National Museum, Stockholm

BAIGNEUSE ON A ROCK, 1892; 32″ × 25″, Collection of Durand-Ruel, Paris

STILL LIFE WITH CUP, 1905
7″ × 10″, Private Collection, Paris

ODALISQUE, 1914; 24″ × 34″, Collection of Ph. Gangnat, Paris

HEAD OF A GIRL (Pastel Study), 1890; 20″ × 12″, Private Collection, Paris

The Hat Trimmed with Flowers, 1897

Ingres became his new ideal. It was just as if, after a ballet, the warm, colourful lights of the performance were suddenly replaced by the cold lights of the auditorium, and the spectators did not hesitate to show their disappointment. The circle of Renoir enthusiasts was horrified, his rich patrons turned away from him, and by the Impressionists, for whom Ingres was on the same level as Antichrist, he was treated as a deserter.

In the *Portrait of Thérèse Bérard*, painted in 1879, one can already sense a cooling-off despite all the magic of the delicate glaze on the face and clothes, a cooling-off, however, which increases the psychological depth of the portrait, and which, as one may well predicate on the grounds of several other group portraits of the Bérard family, is even completely consistent with the spirit and character of the sitter. Here we are again reminded of a painting on enamel. Delicate transitional tones link the softly luminous areas, and the compact silhouette in front of a neutral background classifies the work as a conventional portrait. The *Lady with Veil*, too, differs, as far as colour is concerned, from the works of previous years. The delicate pastel shades hardly recall the past at all, and the

Rhone and Saone,
Red Chalk, 1910 Collection of Durand-Ruel, Paris

plane composition of the picture, the conspicuous emptiness of the right half, point rather to Japanese influences, which indeed was rife everywhere after the World Exhibition in Paris in 1867, with its Oriental pavillions. Bracquemond, Whistler, and Degas collected Japanese art and Oriental bijoux and many of their works show Eastern influences, and Toulouse-Lautrec's posters of the nineties are unthinkable without Utemaro and Hokusai. Renoir himself did not like the subtle colour harmonies of the Japanese woodcuts, but that does not exclude the possibility that in his new uncertainty he borrowed his pastel shades from the Japanese. It would be quite wrong to fix the date of the beginning of the crisis as early as this. If we had not the visual evidence of his pictures of the following 20 years, we should probably have no misgivings, but the break did not come, in fact, before 1883, and was then much more radical. What, however, is evident from the pictures of the years 1879 and 1880, is a basic change in Renoir's relationship to Impressionism.

This change came after a journey to Italy, during which he visited Venice, Rome, Naples, and Florence. Although, while in Venice, he had absorbed and utilized the magic of Southern colour, the colourfulness of that city on the lagoon and its irridescent atmosphere, during his stays in Rome, Naples, and Florence he only visited the museums, enthused about Raphael, and discovered the Pompeian frescoes for himself. In his pictures from Venice, *Gondola on the Canale Grande* and *St. Mark's Square*, he once more pulled out all the stops: the surface shimmers with glorious colour, the brush seems to have been riotously flurried across the canvas, to transform the town into a fantastic mirage. That was the last feast, exuberant, intoxicated, and already somewhat unreal. We no longer participate with all our senses as we did in *The*

Shepherdess Study 1903; Red Chalk

Boating Party, where our eyes could pleasurably flirt with each patch of colour. Here coloured veils have interposed. The curtain is about to fall.

From Venice Renoir went on to Rome and studied Raphael's frescoes; their beauty made a deep impression on him. The old conflict of line versus colour, which Renoir, working with his friends, had decided in favour of colour ten years before, began in him anew, and he prepared himself to take on the heritage of Ingres, the great French master of the line: the heritage which, with the Impressionists, he had up to now denied. Now he was able to draw upon earlier experiences, his meeting, for example, with one of Ingres' pictures, the portrait of a woman which hung in the Louvre next to the « Jewish Wedding » by Delacroix, which he was copying. Even at that time he sensed the clarity of the composition and the beauty of the line. Ingres remained his secret, unavowed love, until it finally became apparent under the influence of the Raphael frescoes. The question of why this change took place calls for an answer. The artist gave an answer to this question to Vollard, who recorded it in his biography of Renoir, as follows: « I had followed Impressionism to the utmost limits, and was forced to come to the conclusions that I could neither paint nor draw. I had reached a dead-end ». Perhaps this is the first place in Renoir's development where the word « genius » may be applied without reservation. Remembering the late works of Pissarro and Monet in which the « limits of Impressionism » are sometimes painfully obvious, one is deeply impressed by the power of a genius which was able to guide the artist through difficult years of struggle and search, to new pastures. Here, too, there are crescendoes and climaxes, but there is always a slow but steady overall growth.

Thus there is no real break to be seen even after the Italian journey. With the impression of Raphael's work fresh on his mind he painted while he was still in Italy a *Blonde Bather* whose gleaming, voluptuous body has the summarily painted sea as background. Here he naively combines Ingres and Raphael and creates a being in whom the joie de vivre of the south is coupled with the coolness of the north. But that is presumably the only nude that he painted on the journey. Having returned to the South of France, he spent February 1882 recuperating from the violence of the Italian light, in L'Estaque, where he met Cézanne, and a few landscapes were produced in the mild climate of the Côte d'Azur. *L'Estaque*, in the Boston Museum, is an example. Here Renoir draws upon his experiences of the seventies: blue-violet shadows on the ground in the wood, bright touches of sun in the green-blue grass. Cézanne appears to have had no influence on Renoir's landscape painting at that time. There is none of the tectonic severity, none of the articulation in small rectangular patches of colour, already used by Cézanne at that time in the composition of his pictures. A charming coastal landscape, perhaps a little overcolourful on the whole, spreads itself out behind the framework of trees and branches in the foreground: effective Mediterranean magic. One would be much more justified in discovering Cézanne's sponsorship in the still-life with the *Mediterranean Fruits* (1881). This picture is not a piece of colourful, atmospheric gossamer, but a well-composed collection of 24 different fruits, clearly distinguished from one another by their drawing and colour. And the colour already has something of the dryness of Cézanne's pictures, and appears to have been applied with rough brush-strokes. The picture is dated 1881, however, that is, earlier than the meeting. But this question is, after all, unimportant, compared with the fact that here the form is consolidating and the colours are being used again more objectively, and this might just as well have been brought about by the impressions gathered in the museums in Italy as by the influence of a contemporary's painting.

Renoir brought another very important asset back with him from Italy: enthusiasm for fresco. How weary he must have been of Impressionism, that his eyes were capable of being opened to the beauty of Raphael's frescoes and the grandness of his composition. The first

68

Head of a Woman; Charcoal Drawing

Woman Bathing 1883; Red Chalk

results of his experiences in Rome were a few pictures in large format from the year 1883, in which he takes up again the beloved Impressionist motif of dancing in the open air, but now completely brought into line with his new conception. *Dance at Bougival*: here we again have the coffee-garden under shady trees, as in *Moulin de la Galette*, the young snub-nosed thing at the table, chatting with the cavaliers from *The Boating Party*. In front of the lightly painted background, however, is the statuesque figure of Suzanne Valadon, a very popular model of that day, pupil of Degas and later independent painter, and mother of Utrillo; next to her, her dancing partner, for whom Edmond, Renoir's brother, was the model. This work already incorporates some mural elements. The background, despite all the Impressionist speckledness, is so muted in colour that the dancing couple, painted in large areas and with strong contours, takes on great prominence. The aim at a decorative effect, with the pyramidal structure rising from the great width below up to the dancer's yellow hat, should, however, not be mistaken. The girl, clinging to her rough partner in the waltz, is one of the most delightful of Renoir's

Coco Painting, Red Chalk; about 1906

creations, and one feels that the painter not only found it easy, but positively enjoyed painting her in such a large format. In a single stream of movement the lines sweep up from the swinging skirt to the red scarf which in turn leads to the chin, from where the movement opens into the roundness of the face. The man is much stiffer and clumsier; the contours are unwieldy, and the dark blue of the jacket and trousers is dead and dry. It is significant that these first symptoms of crisis in Renoir's painting should appear in the male figure, but not yet in the female, whose grace and charm still so fascinated the painter that he was once again able to overcome all his artistic scruples and uncertainty. And if there was anything that was also later constantly to save Renoir from the crisis, it was the natural magical quality that he could sense in women and children.

With *Dance in the Town*, although it was painted in the same year, we have already reached the dry period. The luminous quality has gone from the colours, the volatile, coloured veils of his earlier pictures seem to have been driven off by a gust of cold air, and the forms are sharply distinguished from one another as in the rarefied air of high mountains. The colours are almost academically smooth, although there is a charming duet for blue and green. Mural ideas have a stronger effect in this picture, and the economical colouring of the large areas is again influenced by Japanese coloured woodcuts. This Eastern art, however, did not have a lasting influence on Renoir; he only made use of it while he was in search of new creative principles. His hero remained Ingres, whose influence, as *The Umbrellas*, painted in about 1883, shows, had awakened Renoir's interest in the formal qualities of things, and their plastic representation in a three-dimensional setting. The comical shape of the umbrellas, with the formal discord provided by the bent ribs and rounded surfaces on the one hand, and the pointedness

Pencil Study for the Picture on Page 73. Rudolf Martin Collection, Calgary, Alberta, Canada

and sharp ridges of the edges on the other hand, proved such an attraction for Renoir that he based the composition of the picture on it. The spectator's gaze is directed into the background, and upwards through a lane of swaying domes, it then follows the upright figures downwards, only to rise again. Renoir successfully attempted to transfer the centre of gravity into the upper quarter, and thus, as it were, to « hang » the picture from that point: a reversal of the normal principle of composition, which places the basis of the picture in the lower half. It is still a completely moot point whether Renoir arrived at this unusual solution by experimenting with such abstract principles of composition, or whether the idea was simply suggested to him by the particular shape of the umbrellas. In the following year, however, he began work on a picture whose complicated composition is the result of countless sketches, both of details and of the composition as a whole: *The Bathers* (*Grandes Baigneuses*), Tyson collection — the artistic and stylistic climax of the dry period. The picture has an almost programmatic character. The Impressionist technique, which is still used for the two children in the right foreground in the picture *Umbrellas*, plays nothing more than a very minor role in the landscape in the background of *Girls Bathing* in the collection of Caroll S. Tyson. The wonderful harmony of movement of the four figures, however, is reminiscent of Classicist reliefs, and the many intersections of the legs of the two sitting girls are so balanced that they give the impression of belonging

72

GABRIELLE AND THE RENOIR CHILDREN, 1892-94
22″ × 31″, Collection of Bernheim Jeune, Paris

GABRIELLE ADORNING HERSELF, 1910; 32¼″ × 25¾″, Private Collection, Geneva

WOMAN PLAYING WITH THE GUITAR, 1897; 39″ × 31″, Museum of Art, Lyon

CHRYSANTHEMUMS, 1900
13″ × 16″, Collection of Durand-Ruel, Paris

ROSES IN FRONT OF A BLUE CURTAIN, 1908
19″ × 21″, Collection of Gangnat, Paris

JEAN RENOIR, SEWING, about 1900; 22″ × 18″
Collection of Mr. and Mrs. Martin A. Ryerson, Chicago

◁ WOMAN WITH A RED BLOUSE, about 1890-1895
The Ishibashi Collection, Tokyo

Self-Portrait, 1914; Pencil

SELF-PORTRAIT
◁ 1910; 18″ × 15″, Collection of Pierre Renoir

rather to a choreographic study than to a gay bathing party. With a wonderful open gesture one of the girls draws space into the picture, and at the same time focuses the group into the foreground. The very natural pose of the girl standing up to her waist in the water, lifting up her hair with both hands, allows the picture to fade out towards the background on a weaker accent. The plastic shaping of the bodies, never stiff, never sculptural, is achieved by the mother-of-pearl lustre given to the skin, which, even in the shadowed parts and in the creases, never shows a trace of grey, preserving even there a delicate, lively luminescence. The picture may betray the fact that Renoir took great pains over it, that the composition, and both the application and combination of colours were the result of much experiment — but it is nevertheless completely free of tedium and pedantry. This work, on which Renoir presumably spent three years, was the fulfilment of the promise inherent in *Dance in the Town* — the consolidation of form and line into a monumental gesture.

In his choice of theme, and even in some of the details of posture, Renoir was inspired by a lead relief by Girardon in the Gardens of Versailles, a fact to which Meier-Graefe drew attention; this point is actually of less importance for the understanding of this picture, than for the whole of Renoir's development. The mere realization that Renoir discovered Ingres' art while still emulating his antipode Delacroix, reduces the chasm between the Impressionist and dry periods; still more does the fact that in turning to an earlier, antiquating ideal he once again found contact with his past Impressionist period, during which, after all, he had frequently taken the compositions of the great masters as his inspiration. Florisoone (Renoir, Paris 1938) devotes a whole chapter to Renoir's relationship to tradition, pointing to, among other things, the relationship of some of his pictures with pictures by Rubens, Titian, and Vermeer, and of course to Watteau's *Embarkation to Cythera* and Boucher's *Diana in the Bath*, which Renoir had admired even as a boy. This positive attitude towards tradition is completely consistent with his remark, recorded by Vollard: « I was only myself when I could study in museums ». Even if it should not be taken literally, it is nevertheless no less than a reverent recognition of the artistry of the *Old Masters*, who, unaffected by short-lived modern styles, always remained a timeless and valuable example for him. This recognition also includes, in Renoir's case, the painting technique, which had once been thrown overboard in the general abandonment of tradition by the Impressionists. Because of his training, and experience in porcelain painting, Renoir, in contrast to his friends, felt that he owed something to traditional craftsmanship; for him, the durability of the canvas, its expert priming, the neat application of paint, and careful experimenting to discover the percentage of oil most suitable for a paint, were an essential part of the quality of a picture. Albert André (Renoir, Paris 1919) collected remarks of Renoir's concerning his art, and they show that he was an artist who thought very conscientiously about problems of craftsmanship. One of these remarks was: « I prefer a kind of painting which is fat and oily, and as smooth as possible. That is why I love oils so much. In order to achieve the results I have always desired, I have tried every kind of technique... I have tried painting with dots, in order to obtain better transition from one tone to the other; but this technique results in a rough surface, and I don't like that very much... » When a picture « is painted with this pointillist technique, I am always tempted to strike my matches on it. Apart from that, dust settles in the interstices and changes the tone values. A picture should be able to survive all varnishes, all dirt, and all the maltreatment which time and restorers can bring ».

This attitude of Renoir's towards the work of art — so foreign to the Impressionists — is also based on his study of Cennini's *Tract on Painting*, which he came across in 1883, and which he studied particularly with regard to the technique of fresco painting and the old paint recipes. This purely theoretical knowledge was aptly supplemented by his studies in Italy, where he studied the technique of the frescoes of the 15th century. Renoir now approaches his work very carefully, he paints out, scrapes the paint off, and begins again; he frequently makes new sketches and traces them on to the canvas. He never thought much of the Impressionist conviction that the genuine work of art could only come into being by a lightning-like reproduction of the first impression. But now he becomes over-careful and even uncertain, so that it is actually only at this time, that is, after the painting of the *Bathing Girls* in 1886, that one can really speak of a crisis. The transition from the domination of colour to the domination of the line had taken place painlessly and without hiatus, whereas he found the return to colour in the late eighties and the nineties hard. Often he lacked the courage to put a single dab of colour on the canvas, and even felt it necessary to go to the neighbouring studio of a fashionable painter for advice. One is shocked by the shrill, poster-like red and green of *La Coiffure* of 1888. Parts of the canvas might almost have been painted by a house-painter,

Woman at Her Toilet, 1916, Red Chalk

and the delicate pink of the seated girl's dress, a pink, delightful nuances of which so often appear in his later works, where it adorns voluptuous female bodies, here has an unpleasant obtrusiveness. Despite all the transformation of form and colour, however, the female body retains its natural grace even here. The somewhat coquettish turn of the head which does not try to evade the carefully working hands, but nevertheless wants to be seen at its advantage — en face — was caught by the eye of a painter who could not be distracted from nature however engaged he was by problems of form and theory of art. Nevertheless there are pictures which lack even these qualities, and in which the uncertainty is as shockingly obvious as it is in the family portrait of 1896 (Merion, U.S.A.) with the painter's wife, his two sons Jean and Pierre, the nanny, Gabrielle, and a girl from the neighbourhood. The colours are dull, the forms are doughy rather than soft. Sometimes it seems as if the contours cannot contain the heavy masses of colour, which spread and become bloated. The figures stand stiffly and clumsily next to one another, and the composition lacks all spontaneity. For the first time the people in Renoir's pictures are posing; even if they had done so in previous years he had always been able to give them a natural composure and charm in the work of art. This creative power seems to have failed him in some of the works he painted before the turn of the century. It would be unfair to the artist to conceal these undeniable temporary lapses. To do that would be to belittle the severity of the battle which he had to fight, and detract from the greatness of his victory over the crisis. Now and then there are happy moments when a work like *Baigneuse on a Rock* of 1892 was produced. The skin may no longer have the delicate freshness of the early Impressionist nudes, nor the enamel-like glaze of the eighties, but light plays a creative part in the shaping of the body, it has penetrated it and illuminates the breast and arms from within, giving it the appearance of Parian marble under a Greek sky. The won-

Dancing Girl with Tambourine

derful, artlessly coquettish gesture of the left hand, too, makes up for much that is unnatural and artificial in these years, and shows that feminine beauty can still make the painter forget all his scruples and open the way to naively great creations.

One of these great creations was a meadow landscape with two young girls in the foreground, painted between 1890 and 1894. With this picture Renoir had already taken a decisive step away from his linear style, had opened form to colour again, and had apparently returned to Impressionism; but only apparently, for the invaluable gains of the past years were by no means relinquished. The approximately 15 years older picture *Woman with Parasol* in Boston, from Renoir's Impressionist period, with a similar motif, makes an enlightening comparison. In a comparison of this kind we are not interested in differences in quality, but in the fact that light and colour have a different meaning in each picture. In the earlier work the light comes from an outside source, the sun, and despite all the freedom that Renoir allows himself in the use of broad brush strokes, the illuminated and shadowed parts are quite distinct from one another, — the large splashes of sun in the grass, and the play of light and shadow on the woman's dress. Strong contrasts are achieved by the use of tones ranging from white to a dark, almost black, green; and yet, how much poorer in light is this picture than the landscape with the two girls: here it is unnecessary for an outside source of light to illuminate the scenery and bring the colours to life, for even the darkest green in the trees and the reddish brown of the hair is still as bright as if the paint were luminescent. Renoir also no longer needs the light-dark effects for the composition of a picture. On the basis of his experience during the Ingres period he gives the picture a simple and firm structure: the upright trunks of the sitting girls and the groups of trees on both sides are rhythmically balanced against one another. The prominent figure in the foreground, which takes up a great deal of space, balances the cluster of trees on the right, whereas the half-hidden bright figure of the girl in profile formally corresponds to the delicate tree on the left of the picture. There is none of the fortuitousness, the brusque overlappings, the excerptive quality of the Impressionists; but none of the smoothness and austerity of form, and none of the uncertainty of the colouring of the period of crisis, either. The structure of the picture is retained, but it no longer gives the impression of being dependent on a pencilled outline: It is simply there, without any conscious thought. It is the result of a self-imposed hard asceticism, during which Renoir renounced colour to gain mastery of form. Soon afterwards there was the dangerous period in which the newly acquired force of form got out of control when he tried to fill it with colour again. Finally he overcame the weakness, but only with the aid of his beloved motifs: girls bathing, or against a country background, or with children. The secret of this development can hardly be grasped rationally, it is as though a memory of happy times, which had been overshadowed by hard, bitter years, had now been recaptured slowly under the influence of a simple melody from his youth. Thus there are scarcely any pictures of children by Renoir, even from the period of crisis, in which he does not effortlessly succeed in reproducing their apple-cheeked freshness and delicacy. Renoir covered many yards of canvas with the faces of children and young girls — there are countless portraits just of his sons Pierre and Jean, and later especially of Coco, whom he painted at every imaginable occupation. These motifs accompany Renoir throughout his life. There are often several of them, lightly sketched, in one picture. It is as if he sought recreation in these gentle exercises from the strain of his great compositions. Flower and fruit still-lifes play a similar role. The chrysanthemums of 1900 make one forget all the past wrestling with theoretical problems. Red, in all its many nuances, surges across the picture, mixes with green and white to form a wild maelstrom of colour which seems about to swirl out of the frame. A song of praise to nature, her riches, beauty, and fertility. And these three things remain Renoir's main themes until the day of his death.

Renoir's outward life developed particularly successfully from 1886-1900: the very years of his artistic crisis. Nearly every winter he was able to spend a few years in the South of France. He hated the winter, and painted only one winter picture; he once called snow « nature's scab ». In the summer he returned to Paris with his wife and children and the nanny Gabrielle. There are countless pictures of Gabrielle, who was his model for many years: after bathing, combing her hair, with his children, in country clothes, reading. The picture *Gabrielle with the Rose* in the Louvre shows her coarse beauty. Here he has hung a blouse loosely around her, whom he had so often represented in the nude, in order to contrast the lustre of her skin with the dull white of the material. Once Renoir had found a model whose skin satisfied his artistic ideals, he did not like to part with her again. Thus Gabrielle stayed for many years in his household. The brother of the collector Caillebotte, who was a frequent guest of Renoir's, once said after a dinner: « Extraordinary, I never get a fish soup at home like the one I get at the Renoirs'... And yet I have a proper cook... The only thing that is expected of a cook at Renoir's that she should have a skin that looks well in the light... »

Now Renoir also had considerable success with the public, especially as a result of his exhibition at Durand-Ruel's in 1892; in the same year he was even able to record his first sale of a picture to the State. When, however, in 1894, as executor of his dead friend Caillebotte, he offered Caillebotte's collection of Impressionist painting to the State, he was to meet with only reluctant, and partial acceptance. And that collection included masterpieces by Degas, Manet, and Cézanne. Henri Roujon, the then Director of the Academy, accepted only a few pictures by Degas and Manet, and only one of Renoir's, *Moulin de la Galette*; Cézanne he rejected completely. However, Renoir no longer needed to worry about the recognition of his own art, especially after his second successful exhibition at Durand-Ruel's in 1896. He was 55 years old, could look back on great achievements, and feel the power and passion to strive for new goals ever increasing within him. He lived happily in the circle of his family; and now that he was assured of financial security by the regular sale of his works, he was able to buy a house near Essoyes not far from Paris.

There he suddenly suffered a heavy attack of rheumatism in 1898, but was able to fight it off by taking the waters at Aix-les-Bains. In the following years, however, his illness became worse, travelling became painful, and he was finally confined to an invalid's chair. The illness, no doubt a kind of rheumatism of the joints, affected his whole body, he grew thin, his face became emaciated. Finally fate delivered him a last, terrible blow, in that the disease crippled his hands. This misfortune affected both the man and the artist equally — and both emerged from the trial with superhuman greatness. Vollard records how Renoir, during the time when his illness was already very advanced, considered himself lucky, and overcame the difficulties and pain with a humour that put everybody else to shame. The man mastered this life with humour, the artist — with his art.

His works become more and more sure, one might almost say classical. *The Church at Cagnes* of 1905: green, yellow ochre, and blue, and a few vertical lines which offset the oblique lines of the roof, are the components of the picture. There is no longer any complicated directing of the gaze. From left and right the eye is led to the front of the church and then upwards, following the giant cypresses. The people in the church square have apparently been only summarily painted in, and yet the few dabs of colour suffice to characterize every single person even to their clothes. Renoir also achieved classical greatness in his still-lifes which, however, were never cool or austere. One only has to look at the few strokes of the brush which sufficed for the underside of the saucer in *Still-Life with Cup* (1905) and compare this with *Mediterranean Fruits* of 1881, which then suddenly appear rather ostentatious. The underside of the saucer's edge alone has more artistic qualities than all the colourful fruits together.

Drinking Child; Red, Black, and White Chalk 20″ × 24″. Collection of Harry A. Woodruff, New York

The surface of the table is reflected, and so is the green of the plant on the right, and only an occasional gleam of the porcelain's own colours, blue and white, shows through. Everything is simpler, quieter, and at the same time richer. It is a deeply moving experience if, when looking at Renoir's late pictures, one suddenly recalls the fact that at the time when he transferred these paradisiac visions onto canvas he was already suffering so much from his illness that he could no longer grasp the brush properly, but had to slide it between his crippled fingers. Two self-portraits from the year 1910 show the physically broken man with his wasted face — overwhelming confessions of a man tortured by all the pains of age, but unwaveringly working on and remaining true to his vocation throughout agonizing days and years until the end.

It was in this badly handicapped condition that he painted his most mature works in Cagnes, where he lived towards the end of his life on his small estate *Les Collettes*. Once again it becomes clear how smoothly his creative development progressed. It is as though the genius of his art had postponed this trial until it was incapable of damaging his creative powers. It came at a time when he no longer needed direct contact with nature. Saturated with everything which his eyes could absorb he had long since considered painting in the open air unnecessary, even troublesome, because the direct sunlight affected too strongly the degrees of brightness on palette and canvas. Pure landscapes had gradually disappeared from his painting, and he now almost entirely restricted himself to representing the nude female body. He never painted without a model — that he had learned from Diaz — but he scarcely looked at her any longer; the visions appeared before his inner eye, and found their way onto the canvas.

The works of the last ten years, up to his peaceful death on 3rd December 1919, at the age of 78, are completely devoid of weight, are no longer earthbound. They seem to be visions from another, sun-bright world: playful, nude girls in a rural setting, or on the banks of a river, and *Bathing Girls* in endless variety. His palette, which, after the « dry » period with its cobalt blue and its earthy colours, had at first appeared to have become richer — it then included madder lake, cinnabar, brownish red, yellow ochre, Naples yellow, chrome green, green earth, Cobalt blue, ivory, black, and white — is now limited to a few colours only — cinnabar, ochre, Naples yellow, black, and some white. With these colours, however, he created works which no longer prompt the question of how they were « made », or pose problems of technique and style; one recognizes these pictures, in which contours of people and environment are blurred and everything is joined in a concord of colour, as manifestations of a pantheistic philosophy. It is after all completely unimportant that the picture from 1913 in the Rosenberg collection should be called *The Washerwomen*. For it is after all not the occupations — the washing, rinsing, and wringing —, however explicitly they may be described, which fascinated the painter, but the colourful, lively scene on both sides of the stream. Here we once more have the Rococo pastoral scene as an iconographic basis. With only a slight alteration of the attributes we should have here a gay open-air party; a bathing party by the water, on the left bank two women dancing, in the right foreground a mother with her child, picnicking. And even the stone caryatid, invariably to be found in the background of an 18th century fête galante is here, in the shape of a washerwoman, balancing her basket on her head with nonchalant grace. If the joy of living is heightened here by an occupation, by movement, in other pictures it is deepened by the feeling of stillness, by the consonance with nature in which the figures find themselves: *Two Women with a Young Girl in a Landscape* (Melet-Lauvin collection). This consonance is not the result of a romantic, prodigal abandonment of oneself to nature as to something different and alien. These female figures have their roots in the soil, are themselves nature, and have the natural beauty of everything that grows. The nude female figures in Renoir's late pictures, also, whether they are in a forest setting, by lakes or rivers, like the *Bathing Women* (National Gallery, Stockholm), or in a room like the *Odalisque* (Private Collection, Paris) have this same naturalness. They are not undressed, for these natural bodies appear never to have known clothes. Their nudity is their natural clothing, as the fur is to the animal, the bark to the tree. Even there, where the erotic element might be present — in the partly exposed, voluptuous shoulder and neck of the *Woman, Tying her Shoes* (1918), one of Renoir's last works, it is nevertheless just as remote as it would be in a landscape. But his women and girls are, however, always blooming, lively creatures, possessing all the beauties of this world; it is true, though, that they do not enjoy life's pleasures on this earth, but in the lustrous regions of a paradisiacal innocence — or, in plain words, in the paintings of Renoir.

Renoir worked hard throughout his life, and now that he was confined to an invalid's chair he worked harder than ever; he had been thrifty with time in order to be able to create the great number of his masterpieces. He even at one time, when he was given hope of curing his illness, refused to do so for the sake of his art. Vollard tells of Renoir's meeting with the famous doctor, Henri Gautiez: « As a result of Doctor Gautiez' treatment Renoir succeeded in taking a few steps without assistance. And when the doctor told him that with daily exercises and by the utmost concentration of his will-power... 'But', interrupted the painter, 'and my painting?' — And Renoir sat down in his chair once more, never to leave it again ».

BIOGRAPHICAL DATA

1841   Born on 25th February into the poor and large family of a tailor in Limoges.

1845   Family moves to Paris (Rue d'Argenteuil).

1849   Attends the Ecole Commune; the teacher of singing, Charles Gounod, awakens his interest in music.

1854   Apprentice in a porcelain factory; later he paints fans and curtains. Frequent visits to the Louvre.

1862   Enters the Ecole des Beaux-Arts, and, with Monet, Sisley, and Bazille attends Gleyre's studio.

1863   Leaves Gleyre's studio, studies in the Louvre with Fantin-Latour.

1864   Meets Diaz while painting in the Fontainebleau woods. Exhibits his academic picture « La Esmeralda » in the Salon, later destroys it.

1865   Paints with Sisley and Marlotte. Exhibits two pictures in the Salon.

1866   Paints « Le Cabaret de la Mère Anthony » (Stockholm) at Marlotte. Rejected by the Salon, despite Corot's and Daubigny's support.
In the spring paints with Monet in Paris. Works in Basille's studio.

1867   « Diana Hunting » rejected by the Salon.

1868   « Lise » accepted by the Salon and favourably received by Thoré-Buerger, the critic. Paints a ceiling in Prince Bibesco's villa.

1869   Paints the same themes as Monet in Bougival: Canotiers, La Grenouillière. With his model Lise at Ville d'Avray.

1870   « La Baigneuse » and « Femme d'Alger » accepted by the Salon. A. Houssaye writes enthusiastic notices. Called up to serve in the 10th Light Cavalry Regiment at Bordeaux. Portraits of his captain, Darras, and his wife.

1871   Return to Paris during the Commune. Excursions to Louvecienne and Bougival.

1872   Studio in Rue Notre-Dame-des-Champs. Visits to Monet in Argenteuil. Paints « Le Quai Malaquai » and « Le Pont-Neuf », and others, in Paris. Is introduced to Duret by Degas.

1873   Meets Durand-Ruel who from now on sells Renoir's pictures. Fits out a large studio in Rue Saint-Georges.

1874   Exhibits 7 pictures in the Impressionist Exhibition at Nadar's. Friendship with Caillebotte. Death of his father.

1875   Unsuccessful auction in the Hotel Drouot (pictures by Renoir, Monet, Sisley, and Berthe Morisot). Meets Choquet.

1876   Exhibits 15 pictures in the 2nd Impressionist Exhibition. Studio in Rue Cortot, Montmartre. Paints « The Swing » and « Le Moulin de la Galette ». Beginning of his friendship with the Charpentiers, the Daudet family, and Jeanne Samary.

1877   Exhibits 22 pictures in the 3rd Impressionist Exhibition. Portrait of Jeanne Samary.

1878   Stays at Pourville near Dieppe. Paints the large portrait « Mme Charpentier and her Children » (Metropolitan Museum).

1879   Great success of the picture « Mme Charpentier » in the Salon. Exhibition in the rooms of the magazine « La Vie Moderne ». Makes friends with Paul Bérard, who often invites him to Wargemont, his estate near Berneval (Normandy). Drawings for « La Vie Moderne ».

1880   Growing doubts about his own painting. Begins « The Boating Party ». Studio in Rue de Norvins. Summer at Berneval.

1881   In spring journey to Algiers, in July to Wargemont, in autumn to Italy to see Raphael's works. Enthusiastic about Venice; visits the museums in Rome and Florence; very impressed by the Pompeian frescoes.

1882   Portrait of Richard Wagner (Louvre) in Palermo. Exhibits 25 pictures in the 7th Impressionist Exhibition.

1883   With Monet in Marseille and Genoa. Visits Cézanne in L'Estaque. Paints « The Dance » (model S. Valadon) at Guernesey.

1884   Paints in Paris and La Rochelle. In search of a new style he gives up Impressionism.

1885   Birth of his son Pierre. Sketches for « Les Grandes Baigneuses », Stays at Wargemont and, with Cézanne, at La Roche-Guyon.

1886   Takes part in the Impressionist Exhibition (organised by Durand-Ruel) in New York, in the Exhibition of the XX in Brussels, and in the « Exposition Internationale » at Georges Petit's.

1888   Stays at Cézanne's at Jas de Bouffan and, during the winter, at Martigues.

1889   At Cézanne's at Montbriand near Aix.

1890   Studio in Boulevard de Clichy. Exhibits for the last time in the Salon. Visits Berthe Morisot at Mézy.

1891   Travels to Tamaris with Teodor de Wyzews. Short trip to Spain.

1892   First sale of a picture to the State. With Gallimard to Spain. Stays at Pont-Avon. Wall-paintings for Durand-Ruel. Gangnat buys his first Renoir pictures.

1893   Birth of Jean (second son). Winter at Beaulieu, summer at Pont-Avan. The nanny, Gabrielle, becomes his favourite model.

1894   Death of Caillebotte, who leaves his collection to the State. Renoir is made executor. Studio in Rue Tourlaque.

1895   Stays in Provence. Travels to London and Holland.

1896   Exhibition at Durand-Ruel's. Travels to Bayreuth.

1897   Through Renoir's efforts Caillebotte's collection is accepted by the museums (the collection includes 6 Renoirs). Stays at Berneval.

1898   Buys a house at Essoyes as summer residence.

1899   His health deteriorates. Rheumatism compels him to spend the winter in the south (Cagnes).

1900   Stays at Grasse, Saint-Laurent-les-Bains, and Louveciennes. Is made Chevalier de la Légion d'Honneur.

1901   Birth of Claude (« Coco »), the third son. Takes the waters at Aix-les-Bains.

1902   Settles in Le Cannet.

1903   Spends the winter at Le Cannet, the summer at Essoyes. Rents « Le Collettes » near Cagnes.

1904   New attacks of rheumatism. Takes the waters at Bourbonne-les-Bains. Successful retrospective exhibition in the Autumn Salon.

1905-9   Rheumatism aggravated by complications.

1910   Improvement in health enables him to travel to Munich to Thurneyssen.

1911   Buys a car for the regular journeys between Essoyes, Paris, and Cagnes.

1912   Paralysis of the arms and legs. Presentation of the « Croix d'Officier ».

1913   Large exhibition at Bernheim's.

1914   Outbreak of war. Pierre and Jean wounded. Death of his wife.

1919   Visit to the Louvre after spending the summer at Essoyes. Dies on 3rd December at Cagnes.

BIBLIOGRAPHY

CATALOGUES AND ARTISTS' ENCYCLOPEDIAS

Catalogue of the *Renoir-Exhibition, Bernheim*, Paris, March 1913; foreword by Octave Mirabeau; 40 illustrations.

DELTEIL, L.: *Pissarro, Sisley, Renoir. Le peintre-graveur illustré*, Vol. XVII; Paris, 1923.

Auction Catalogue of the *Coll. Gangnat*, Paris, June 1925; foreword by R. de Flers and E. Faure; 161 illustrations.

ANDRE, A. and ELDER, M.: *L'Atelier de Renoir*, Paris, Bernheim, 1931; 2 Voiumes, 716 illustrations.

Catalague of the Renoir Exhibition in the *Museé de l'Orangerie*, Paris 1933; foreword by P. Jamot, Catalogue by Ch. Sterling; 150 numbers.

Catalogue of the Exhibition *L'Oeuvre gravé, l'oeuvre sculpté, aquarelles et dessins de Renoir*, Galerie des Beaux-Arts, Paris 1934; foreword by R. Cogniat and A. Vollard.

Catalogue of the Exhibition: *Renoir, Special exhibition of his paintings*; Metropolitan Museum, New York, 1937; foreword by H. B. Wehle.

Kuenstlerlexikon: Thieme-Becker, Vol. 28, Leipzig 1934; article « Renoir » by W. Grohmann; biography, the most important works, and a comprehensive bibliography.

Dictionnaire critique et documentaire des peintres, sculpteurs, dessinateurs et graveurs; Bénézit, Vol. 7, article « Renoir » by D. Huisman; biography, the most important works, extensive list of auction and sales prices.

Allgemeines Lexikon der bildenden Kuenstler des XX. Jahrhunderts; published by H. Vollmer, Vol. IV, Leipzig (in preparation).

MONOGRAPHS

MEIER-GRAEFE, J.: *Renoir*, Munich, R. Piper, 1911; (100 illustrations); Leipzig, Klinkhardt und Biermann, 1929 (417 illustrations).

MIRABEAU, O.: *Renoir*, Paris, 1913 (also contains excerpts from writings of Renoir by his contemporaries).

VOLLARD, A.: *Tableaux pastels, dessin par P. A. Renoir*, Paris, A. Vollard, 1918.

VOLLARD, A.: *La vie et l'oeuvre de Pierre-Auguste Renoir*, Paris, A. Vollard, 1919; enlarged edition Paris, Crés, 1920; German edition Berlin, Cassirer, 1924; English edition London, Knopf, 1926.

ANDRE, A.: *Renoir*, Paris, Crès, 1919; enlarged edition 1928.

JEAN, R.: *Dix aquarelles, sanguines et pastels d'Auguste Renoir*. Geneva and Paris, Georg, 1920.

RIVIERE, G.: *Renoir et ses amis*, Paris, Floury, 1921.

FOCSA, F.: *Renoir*, Paris, Rieder, 1923 (« Les Maitres de l'Art Moderne »).

DURET, T.: *Renoir*, Paris, Bernheim-Jeune, 1924.

COQUIOT, G.: *Renoir*, Paris, Albin Michel, 1925.

BASLER, A.: *Pierre-Auguste Renoir*, Paris, Gallimard, 1928 (« Les Peintres Francais Nouveaux »).

ROGER-MARX, C.: *Renoir*, Paris, Floury, 1933; (« Anciens et Modernes »).

FLORISOONE, m.: *Renoir*, Paris, Hyperion, 1938.

TERRASSE, CH.: *Cinquante portraits de Renoir*, Paris, Floury, 1941.

GRABER, H.: *Auguste Renoir nach eigenen und fremden Zeugnissen*, Basle, 1943.

DRUCKER, M.: *Renoir*, Paris, Tisné, 1944; new edition 1955.

HAESAERTS, P.: *Renoir sculpteur*, Brussels, Hermes, 1947.

RAYNAL, M.: *Renoir*, Geneva, Skira, 1949.

BAUDOT, J.: *Renoir, ses amis, ses modèles*, Paris, 1951.

PACH, W.: *P.A. Renoir*, New York, Abrams, 1951.

NEMITZ, F.: *Auguste Renoir*, Cologne, Phaidon, 1952.

GAUNT, W.: *P.A. Renoir*, London, 1953.

ROUART, D.: *Renoir, eine biographisch-historische Studie*, Geneva, Skira, 1954.

P. A. Renoir, Aquarelle, Pastelle, und farbige Zeichnungen, Basle, Holbein-Verlag, 1957.

OWN WRITINGS

Article on *L'Art décoratif contemporain* in *L'Impressioniste*, No. 4, 28th April 1877

Letter to Mottez as preface to C. Cennini's *Le livre d'Art*, Paris 1911

Letters to Monet in G. Geffroy's *Monet, sa vie, son oeuvre*, Paris, 1924

Letters to A. André in the *Bulletin des Expositions*, November, December, Braun & Cie, Paris 1932

Letters to Bazille in G. Poulain's *Bazille et ses amis*, Paris 1932

Letters to M. Choquet in *L'Amour de l'Art* (J. Joets), April 1935

Letters to Mme Charpentier and Duret in *L'Amour de l'Art* (M. Florisoone), February 1938

Letters to Durand-Ruel and Octave Maus in L. Venturi's *Les Archives de l'Impressionisme*, Paris - New York 1939

Letters to Berthe Morisot in Denis Rouart's *Correspondance de B. Morisot*, Paris 1952

EXHIBITIONS

1879 Exhibition of the Magazine « La Vie Moderne » (Charpentier), Paris
1883 Durand-Ruel Gallery, Paris
1892 Durand-Ruel Gallery, Paris
1896 Durand-Ruel Gallery, Paris
1902 Durand-Ruel Gallery, Paris
1904 Autumn Exhibition, Salle Renoir, Paris
1912 Durand-Ruel Gallery (Portraits), Paris
1913 Thannhauser Gallery, Berlin
1913 Bernheim-Jeune Gallery, Paris
1914 Durand-Ruel Gallery, New York
1918 Durand-Ruel Gallery, New York
1919 Durand-Ruel Gallery, New York
1920 Durand-Ruel Gallery, New York
1920 Autumn Exhibition, Memorial Exhibition, Paris
1920 Durand-Ruel Gallery, Paris
1921 Exhibition at the National Gallery, Oslo
1921 Durand-Ruel Gallery, Paris
1923 Duret Gallery, Paris
1924 Durand-Ruel Gallery, New York
1927 P. Rosenberg Gallery (50 Renoir choisis parmi les nus, les fleurs, les enfants), Paris
1927 A. Flechtheim Gallery, Berlin
1928 A. Flechtheim Gallery, Berlin
1932 Braun Gallery, Paris

1933 Musée de l'Orangerie (Catalogue of 149 numbers, by Ch. Sterling and P. Jamot), Paris
1934 P. Rosenberg Gallery, Paris
1934 Galerie des Beaux-Arts (Sculptures, Watercolours, Graphic Art; Foreword by A. Vollard and R. Cogniat), Paris
1937 Exhibition at the Metropolitan Museum, (144 Numbers, Foreword by H. B. Wehle), New York
1938 Bernheim-Jeune Gallery (Renoir portraitiste), Paris
1939 Durand-Ruel Gallery, New York
1941 Duveen Brothers Gallery (Renoir Centennial Exhibition), New York
1943 Kunsthalle, Basle
1948 Lefèvre Gallery, London
1950 Wildenstein Gallery, New York
1952 Wildenstein Gallery (139 Paintings, 5 Sculptures; Foreword by H. B. Wehle), New York.
1952 Exhibition at the Musée Municipal, Limoges
1954 Rosenberg Gallery, New York (Works of the Last Twenty Years)
1956 Musée Jenisch, Vevey (Switzerland)
1956 Kunsthalle (54 Paintings from the Collection of Gangnat); Duesseldorf

ILLUSTRATIONS